The Essential Cocktail Book

Classic and Modern Cocktail Recipes For Every Day incl. Gin, Whisky, Vodka, Rum and More

Peter A. Morgan

ISBN - 9798550815779

Table of Contents

Learning how to mix great cocktails is really easy, and it is definitely worth the time. Finally, you will become one of the best bartenders, although your bar will be your kitchen, and your "customers" your family and friends.

Mixing drinks at home is not only fun, but it will also make you save so much money. Besides, you will be able to choose your own ingredients, and experiment with them until you reach the perfect taste.

In this recipe book, you will find all the most useful tips for becoming an expert bartender. We have also picked a few recipes which you can immediately try, to impress all your friends!

The Basics of Bartending

The Definition of "Cocktail"

Before you start mixing drinks, you should understand what a cocktail is. In fact, some beverages are "mixed drinks", while some others meet the definition of "cocktail".

As a general rule, a mixed drink is a combination of two or more ingredients. This is the case of a Rum & Coke.

On the other hand, a cocktail is a combination of liquors, bitters, sweetener, and water or ice.

Once you understand this difference, it will be easier to follow any recipe and to experiment with different ingredients and beverages.

How to Serve Your Cocktail

How do you usually have or serve your drinks? Learning the bar lingo is essential to become the best bartender!

- *"Neat"* is used for drinks which are poured directly from the bottle, with no mixers or ice. This is usually the best way to enjoy the taste of distilled spirits, with no additional flavourings.

- *"Up"* is used to describe drinks which are chilled with either shaken or stirred ice, and then poured into a glass without ice.

- *"Straight Up"* is when the cocktail is stirred with ice, then poured into a glass.

Liquor vs. Liqueur

Liquors are distilled spirits, which have gone through a distillation process and have come out with high alcohol content.

Liqueurs are distilled spirits in which sweetener has been added.

When following a cocktail recipe, you always need to pay attention to these two similar, yet very different, words!

Understanding Your Liqueurs

Liqueurs are distilled spirits used to add flavours to your cocktail. There are several types of liqueurs, from fruity to bitter tastes.

However, the main difference you should be aware of is the one between "*crème*" and "*cream liqueurs*". Crème liqueurs, which name is often written in French, are made with more sugar and have a syrupy texture, although they are not creamy.

On the other hand, cream liqueurs (such as the Irish cream) have a creamy texture and a less sweet aftertaste.

Different Types of Distilled Spirits

There are six types of liquor you can play with to make your marvellous drinks. They are usually known as the "base distilled spirits" because they are often the starting point of many mixed drinks, as well as the foundations for several liqueurs. These are:

- **Gin**, distilled from grains.

- **Brandy**, distilled from grapes or, less often, other fruits.

- **Tequila**, distilled from the agave plant, directly from Mexico.

- **Rum**, made by distilling molasses or sugar, which gave it a distinctive, sweet taste.

- **Whisky**, distilled from fermented grains.

- **Vodka**, distilled from potatoes.

Additional Useful Spirits and Alcoholic Beverages

Mixing a good cocktail is not all about using the six basic liquors. In fact, there are several other spirits and liqueurs which do not go through any distillation process but are still essential for your bartending career.

- Absinthe, an unsweetened spirit, often misclassified as a liqueur.

- Vermouth and other fortified wines. Usually, they are served with a small amount of distilled spirit, to highlight their taste.

- Beers

- Wines

You do not need to have all these spirits and beverages at home. Based on the recipe you are following, some of these ingredients can be replaced. Besides, you are more than encouraged to explore different tastes to change standard recipes a little bit to make them more suitable for your tastes and the ingredients you have access to.

We do not recommend investing in buying all these spirits, especially because some of them can be particularly expensive. You should start by the one you really like and you believe are more versatile, based on the types of cocktails you are going to mix more often.

The Essential Bar Gear

One of the most essential steps of your journey to becoming the best bartender is to build your perfect gear of tools to use to mix your cocktails with. There are several pieces available on the market, and it is easy to get lost and end up buying a bunch of stuff you may never use.

The first thing you should understand is that there is no need to go all out. Unless you are really planning to settle a professional bar in your kitchen, you will only need a few, essential bar tools.

According to some of the most experienced bartenders, all you need to always be ready to make the perfect drink is:

- Bar spoon

- Cocktail shaker

One jigger, to measure all ingredients

- Muddler, to mix creamy ingredients and fruits

- Strainer, unless built into your shaker

How to Choose the Best Cocktail Shaker

Not all cocktails require a shaker. In fact, you can make mixed drinks, such as gin and tonic, even if you don't have this tool at home.

On the other hand, if you really want to master the art of bartending, then investing in a good shaker is essential. Shakers are usually pretty convenient and are important to mix up any great cocktail. Many of them come with see-through walls to show how much spirits you have poured, and to make your mixing process look even cooler!

Learning the Essential Drink Mixing Techniques

Once you have all the ingredients and tools you need, you are ready to start mixing some cocktails. However, you cannot just fill your shaker with some spirits and then call it a drink. In fact, there are several mixing techniques that you must learn and master to become a true bartender. Some of these techniques are very easy, whereas others may require a bit of practice and experience. Don't worry! Day after day, and cocktail after cocktail, your skill will improve and you will soon become an expert bartender!

Basic Bartending Techniques

- **Shaken vs Stirred**. Although these two words are often used interchangeably, they have two very different meanings. You can shake all cocktails who have juices or any flavoured ingredients. Contrarily, you stir drinks which are made of liquor or that need to be poured directly into a glass.

- **Straining cocktails**. Once your cocktail is ready, you shouldn't serve it with the same ice you used to mix it. Straining is thus necessary to make your drinks smoother and more delicious by using fresh ice.

- **"Building" your drink**. Cocktails are usually built directly into the glass they are served in. This is a very easy bartender technique, which will immediately make you look like a professional.

- **Topping a cocktail**. If a recipe asks you to top your cocktail with a certain ingredient, it means that you should fill the glass with it. When topping the glass with more than one ingredient, you must always follow the order specified in the recipe, to make sure that all flavours and colours are layered perfectly.

- **Blending drinks**. This is one of the most important parts of your bartending journey, especially if you love frozen cocktails. Don't forget to use the right amount of ice!

Advanced Bar Techniques

- **Rolling a drink** means that you should pour it from one container to another. Pay attention to never spill the drink outside its glass, and to shake it carefully to not break the chemicals of your spirits.

- **Layering cocktails** is easier than it may seem. All you need to do is to place ingredients on top of one another, creating colourful layers. Don't forget that each ingredient has a different texture and taste, and it is thus important to know all these features when layering them.

- **Muddling drinks**. Some cocktails, such as the mojito, need to be muddled, which means smashed, to bring out all their freshness and aroma. You can muddle all types of fresh and frozen fruits, as well as herbs, spices, and leaves. If you don't have any professional tool to muddle your ingredients, you can just use a wooden spoon.

Finding (and Making) Your Own Ingredients

Mixing a good cocktail is not all about pouring a few spirits and liquors together. In fact, there are other ingredients that you might wish to use, and each of them needs to be of the highest quality to ensure that your cocktail tastes perfect.

The best way to pick the freshest and most delicious ingredients is to make your own. This will also help you save a lot of money!

Don't be afraid. These recipes are very easy to make, and you won't need any professional tool. Besides, some of these ingredients can also be used for other recipes, such as desserts.

Homemade Drink Sweeteners

- **Simple Syrup**. The syrup is used in many cocktails because of its liquid form, which makes it easier to mix and dissolve into drinks. All you need to do is to bring some water to a boil, and then dissolve the sugar into it. If you want, you can add extra flavourings to spice it up.

- **Grenadine**. Grenadine is a pomegranate-flavoured syrup used to make several tequila-based cocktails. To make your delicious grenadine at home, you need to combine sugar and pomegranate juice and bring to a boil. Once ready, add a few dashes of orange flower water, to enhance its aftertaste.

- **Sour Mix**. Also known as "bar mix", this syrup is made with lemon and it is usually added to tropical cocktails like the margarita. There are several ways to make the sour mix at home, but the secret is to always use excellent quality simple syrup. This is when your homemade simple syrup can come in handy!

- **Agave Nectar**. This is a good alternative to simple syrup, although it is not easy to make it at home. The best way is to experiment with different types of agave nectars which you can find on the market until you find the one which works best for you.

♋ **Lime Cordial**. Lime cordial shows that lime juice can be used as a sweetener for several cocktails. To make your own, you need to boil some citric acid, sugar and water. Once you obtain a syrupy mixture, you can flavour it with lime pieces.

The Importance of Ice

What is one of the main ingredients of any excellent cocktail? The ice! It is required to make almost all cocktails and mixed drinks, and it definitely deserves a lot of attention. For example, certain recipes can only be made with fresh ice, meaning that you cannot just use some ice cubes that you happened to have in your freezer. Besides, tap water may not always be the best starting point to make your ice, unless you use a filter.

Better Ice Makes Better Cocktails

Many think that the purpose of ice is just to chill their drink. However, you should never forget that ice is made of water, meaning that this is what it will release into your cocktail, changing its texture and flavour. This addition blends all the drink's flavours perfectly while mellowing the alcohol and any other strong taste, making an overall smoother flavour.

Based on the type of cocktail you want to mix, there are five basic forms of ice:

- **Ice cubes**. Depending on the glasses you are using, you may need different sizes of ice cubes. When in this form, ice releases a significant amount of water into your drinks, so you should be careful to avoid overly diluted beverages.

- **Shaved ice**. This is the same type of ice usually produced by soda fountain machines. It has a very fine texture, perfect to create thick cocktails.

- **Cracked ice**. Cracked ice releases a significant quantity of water into drinks and melts very quickly. This is the best option to make frozen drinks as it works perfectly with the blender blades.

- **Block ice**. If you like to play with different tools and you feel confident enough, you can just buy a large block of ice and create smaller chunks based on your needs. otherwise, you can play with ice blocks to carve ice rings or to garnish larger containers.

- **Ice balls**. Ice balls work exactly like ice cubes, but look cooler. They are perfect for serving whiskey or other on the rocks drinks. Most importantly, ice balls can last for hours before they start melting.

5 Tips to Become an Excellent Bartender

When it comes to becoming a bartender, the golden rule is that practice makes better. If you are looking for a good starting point to kick start your new hobby, here you will find a few tips from the best bartenders!

Learn Something New Every Day

Ideally, you should learn a new drink every day. However, if you don't have time to practice with new beverages every day, you should still dedicate a few minutes to building the foundation of your cocktails' knowledge. For example, you should learn new techniques, or just read new recipes to find some inspiration for your drinks.

Everything in Its Place

Whenever you are ready to mix your drinks, you must have access to anything you may need, from ingredients to the right tools. For this reason, you should always have your own checklist and adequate knowledge of where

everything is. Your working space needs to be in order, always efficient and effective.

Don't Fear Experimentation

At the beginning of your journey as a bartender, you will most likely rely on recipe books. However, once you have learnt the basics, you will be ready to experiment. This will also come in handy when you need to substitute an ingredient with another, or whenever you want to test new recipes and create bespoke drinks for your friends and family.

Never Stop Learning

Of course, bartending is all about practice. However, you should never stop reading new books, and learning new techniques. If you are passionate about bartending, you should always keep up to date with the latest news, ingredients and trends, and learn new tricks every day.

Don't Drink While You Are Mixing

Any professional bartender knows that you must always serve others before serving yourself. Although you may be eager to taste your drinks and share them with your friends and family, you should mix your cocktails only

after others have already been served. You will need a clear mind and no distraction of any sort to focus on the mixing process.

CLASSIC EASY COCKTAIL RECIPES

COSMOPOLITAN

Difficulty: Easy ¦ Kcal: 161 ¦ Carbs: 0 g
Sugars: 10 g ¦ Gluten-Free ¦ Vegan

INGREDIENTS

- 30 ml (1 oz.) cranberry juice
- 15 ml (0.5 oz.) triple sec
- 45 ml (1.5 oz.) lemon vodka
- 10 ml (0.33 oz.) lime juice
- Ice
- Ora zest or lime wedge, to garnish

PREPARATION

1. Shake all ingredients in a cocktail shaker with abundant ice.
2. Pour the drink into a cocktail glass.
3. To make the garnish, wave a piece of orange zest over a lit match. Bend the outer edge of the zest towards the flame to release all the essential orange oils. After a few seconds, drop the zest into your cocktail.

MOJITO

Difficulty: Easy ¦ Kcal: 158 ¦ Carbs: 4.6 g
Sugars: 4.3 g ¦ Vegan

INGREDIENTS

- 60 ml (2 oz.) white rum
- The juice of 1 lime
- Mint leaves
- 1 tsp granulated sugar
- Soda water, to taste
- Mint sprig, to garnish

PREPARATION

1. Muddle the sugar, mint and lime juice in a jug, until the mint is completely crushed.
2. Pour the mint mixture into a tall glass, along with ice cubes.
3. Pour the rum while stirring with a spoon.
4. Fill with soda water.
5. Add additional mint leaves to garnish.

VODKA MARTINI

Difficulty: Easy ¦ Kcal: 155 ¦ Carbs: 0.4 g
Sugars: 0.4 g ¦ Vegan

INGREDIENTS

- 1 tbsp dry vermouth
- 60 ml (2 oz.) vodka
- 1 olive, to garnish
- Lemon peel, to garnish

PREPARATION

1. Combine the dry vermouth and vodka together in a shaker, with some ice.
2. Pour the drink into a chilled martini glass.
3. Add an olive on a cocktail stick or some lemon peel to garnish.

CUBA LIBRE

Difficulty: Easy ¦ Kcal: 159 ¦ Carbs: 10 g
Sugars: 10 g ¦ Gluten-Free ¦ Vegetarian

INGREDIENTS

- 50 ml (1.7 oz.) white rum
- 100 ml (3.4 oz.) cola
- ½ lime, cut into wedges
- Ice cubes

PREPARATION

1. Squeeze the juice from some of the lime wedges into a tall glass.
2. Fill it with ice.
3. Pour the rum and the cola, and stir gently.
4. Drop the remaining wedges into the glass before serving.

CAIPIRINHA

Difficulty: Easy ¦ Kcal: 245 ¦ Carbs: 31 g
Sugars: 30 g ¦ Gluten-Free ¦ Dairy-free ¦ Egg-free ¦ Vegan

INGREDIENTS

- 6 tsp golden caster sugar
- 2 limes, chopped into wedges
- 200 ml (6.8 oz.) cachaça
- Crushed ice
- Additional lime wedges, to garnish

PREPARATION

1. Put the sugar and the lime wedges in a jug. With a muddler or a wooden spoon, mash everything together, making sure that the limes release as much juice as possible. Once you get a syrup, you can discard the lime peel.
2. Pour the syrup and the cachaça into cocktail glasses and top with ice and extra lime wedges.

WHITE RUSSIAN

Difficulty: Easy ¦ Kcal: 246 ¦ Carbs: 9.2 g
Sugars: 9.7 g ¦ Gluten Free

INGREDIENTS

- 60 ml (2 oz.) vodka
- 1 tbsp cream
- 2 tbsp Kahlua
- Ice cubes

PREPARATION

1. Mix all your ingredients together.
2. Serve into a small tumbler with ice cubes.

BLACK RUSSIAN

Difficulty: Easy ¦ Kcal: 204 ¦ Carbs: 8 g
Sugars: 8 g ¦ Gluten-Free ¦ Egg-free ¦ Vegan

INGREDIENTS

- 25 ml (0.85 oz.) coffee liqueur
- 50 ml (1.7 oz.) vodka
- 1 maraschino cherry
- Ice cubes
- Cola, to top up

PREPARATION

1. Pour the coffee liqueur and the vodka into a tumbler, along with ice. Stir gently for about 1 minute.
2. Top with a splash of cold cola (optional)
3. Serve with the cherry on top.

OLD FASHIONED

Difficulty: Easy ¦ Kcal: 191 ¦ Carbs: 7.2 g
Sugars: 7.2 g

INGREDIENTS

- 60 ml (2 oz.) Scotch whisky or bourbon
- 2 tsp sugar syrup
- 1 splash of water
- 2 dashes Angostura bitters
- Orange slice, to garnish
- Maraschino cherry, to garnish
- Soda water

PREPARATION

1. Mix the water, bitters and sugar in a small tumbler.
2. Stir in the whiskey and then fill the glass with ice.
3. Top with a splash of soda.
4. Garnish with the cherry on a cocktail stick and the orange slice before serving.

PIMM'S

Difficulty: Easy ¦ Kcal: 175 ¦ Carbs: 25.5 g
Sugars: 25.3 g

INGREDIENTS

- 600 ml (20.3 oz.) lemonade
- 200 ml (6.8 oz.) Pimm's No. 1
- Mint sprigs, to garnish
- Ice cubes
- Sliced cucumber, to garnish
- Sliced orange, to garnish
- Fresh strawberries, to garnish

PREPARATION

1. Fill a jug with Pimm's, ice, and lemonade.
2. Stir well, and garnish with strawberries, cucumber slices, orange slices, and mint sprigs before serving.

DAIQUIRI

Difficulty: Easy ¦ Kcal: 146 ¦ Carbs: 7 g
Sugars: 7 g ¦ Gluten-Free ¦ Vegan

INGREDIENTS

- 50 ml (1.7 oz.) white rum
- 10 ml (0.3 oz.) sugar syrup
- 25 ml (0.8 oz.) lime juice
- Ice cubes

PREPARATION

1. Mix all the ingredients with a cocktail shaker.
2. Serve with additional ice.

TEQUILA SUNRISE

Difficulty: Easy ¦ Kcal: 92 ¦ Carbs: 8 g
Sugars: 8 g ¦ Gluten-Free ¦ Egg-free ¦ Vegan

INGREDIENTS

- 50 ml (1.7 oz.) tequila
- 2 tbsp grenadine
- 1 tbsp triple sec
- Ice cubes
- The juice of 1 orange
- The juice of ½ lemon
- 1 cocktail cherry

PREPARATION

1. Place the grenadine into the base of one tall glass.
2. Put the triple sec, tequila, fruit juices and ice into a cocktail shaker and shake well.
3. Add ice cubes to the tall glass and then double strain your cocktail into it.
4. Serve with additional ice and garnish with a cherry on a cocktail stick.

SEX ON THE BEACH

Difficulty: Easy ¦ Kcal: 92 ¦ Carbs: 8 g
Sugars: 8 g ¦ Gluten-Free ¦ Egg-free ¦ Vegan

INGREDIENTS

- 50 ml (1.7 oz.) vodka
- 50 ml (1.7 oz.) cranberry juice
- 25 ml (0.85 oz.) peach schnapps
- The juice of 2 oranges
- Glacé cherries to garnish
- Ice cubes
- Orange slices, to garnish

PREPARATION

1. Fill the glasses with the ice cubes.
2. Pour the fruit juices, vodka and the peach schnapps into a large jug. Stir everything together.
3. Pour the mixture into the two glasses and stir once again.
4. Garnish with the cherries and additional orange slices before serving.

BLOODY MARY

Difficulty: Easy ¦ Kcal: 189 ¦ Carbs: 8 g
Sugars: 28 g ¦ Vegan

INGREDIENTS

- 200 ml (6.7 oz.) tomato juice
- 1 tsp sherry vinegar
- 50 ml (1.7 oz.) vodka
- Ice cubes
- 2 tbsp amontillado sherry
- A pinch of salt
- Tabasco, to taste
- Worcestershire sauce, to taste
- Lemon juice
- Celery sticks, to garnish
- Lemon wedges, to garnish
- Pepper, to serve (optional)

PREPARATION

1. Pour the vodka, tomato juice, sherry vinegar and amontillado into a tall glass along with some ice cubes.
2. Season with Tabasco, celery salt and Worcestershire sauce. Add lemon juice to taste.
3. Serve with lemon wedges, celery sticks and freshly ground black (optional).

LONG ISLAND ICED TEA

Difficulty: Easy ¦ Kcal: 212 ¦ Carbs: 16 g
Sugars: 16 g ¦ Gluten-Free ¦ Vegan

INGREDIENTS

- 50 ml (1.7 oz.) London dry gin
- 50 ml (1.7 oz.) vanilla vodka
- 50 ml (1.7 oz.) tequila
- 50 ml (1.7 oz.) triple sec
- 50 ml (1.7 oz.) rum
- 50 ml (1.7 oz.) fresh lime juice
- 500 ml (17 oz.) cola
- 2 limes, cut into wedges
- Ice cubes

PREPARATION

1. Pour all the spirits and liqueurs into a large jug. Add lime juice.
2. Fill ½ of the jug with ice cubes and stir well.
3. Fill the jug with cola and stir once again.
4. Add the lime wedges and serve the cocktail into 4 tall glasses with additional ice cubes.

SANGRIA

Difficulty: Medium ¦ Kcal: 232 ¦ Carbs: 22 g
Sugars: 22 g ¦ Gluten-Free ¦ Vegetarian

INGREDIENTS

- 750 ml (25.4 oz) light red wine
- 200 g (6.8 oz.) red berries, chopped
- ice
- 1 tsp cinnamon
- 3 tbsp caster sugar
- 100 ml (3.4 oz.) Spanish brandy
- 300 ml (10.4 oz.) sparkling water
- 2 lemons, 1 chopped, 1 juiced
- 2 pears, chopped
- 2 oranges, chopped

PREPARATION

1. Put all the chopped fruit in a large bowl along with the cinnamon and sugar. Stir well.
2. Refrigerate overnight, or at least for 1 hour.
3. Fill a jar with ice.
4. Mix the fruit mixture with the wine and the brandy.
5. Top with sparkling water and serve.

ESPRESSO MARTINI

Difficulty: Medium ¦ Kcal: 258 ¦ Carbs: 26 g
Sugars: 25 g ¦ Gluten-Free ¦ Vegan

INGREDIENTS

- 100 ml (3.4 oz.) vodka
- 100 g (3.4 oz.) golden caster syrup
- 50 ml (1.7 oz.) coffee liqueur
- 50 ml (1.7 oz.) freshly brewed espresso
- A few coffee beans, to garnish

PREPARATION

1. Bring the caster sugar to boil in 50 ml (1.7 oz.) of water. Allow the mixture to cool, stirring frequently until you obtain the right consistency for your sugar syrup.
2. Pour 1 tbsp of this sugar into a cocktail shaker with all the other ingredients.
3. Shake well and serve into 2 refrigerated martini glasses.
4. Garnish with additional coffee beans.

MODERN COCKTAILS RECIPES

GIMLET

Difficulty: Easy ¦ Kcal: 294 ¦ Carbs: 40 g
Sugars: 40 g ¦ Gluten-Free ¦ Vegan

INGREDIENTS

- 50 ml (1.7 oz.) London dry gin
- 50 ml (1.7 oz.) lime syrup or lime cordial
- Ice cubes
- 1 slice of lime, to garnish
- 1 edible flower, to garnish (optional)

PREPARATION

1. Leave a coupe glass in the fridge to chill for a while.
2. Pour the lime syrup or cordial into a tall glass with some ice cubes.
3. Add the gin and stir well.
4. Pour the mixture into your chilled glass.
5. Garnish with a slice of lime and an edible flower (optional).

SWEET MANHATTAN

Difficulty: Easy ¦ Kcal: 163 ¦ Carbs: 3 g
Sugars: 3 g ¦ Gluten-Free ¦ Vegetarian

INGREDIENTS

- 25 ml (0.85 oz.) syrup for a jar of maraschino cherries
- 50 ml (1.7 oz.) bourbon
- 2 dashes Angostura bitters
- 25 ml (0.85 oz.) Rosso vermouth
- Ice cubes
- Maraschino cherries to garnish

PREPARATION

1. Stir all ingredients together with a few ice cubes in a mixing glass.
2. Serve into a cocktail glass with additional maraschino cherries.

MANGO AND PINEAPPLE MOJITO

Difficulty: Easy ¦ Kcal: 183 ¦ Carbs: 10 g
Sugars: 8 g ¦ Gluten-Free ¦ Vegan

INGREDIENTS

- 150 ml (5 oz.) white rum
- 600 ml (20.2 oz.) sparkling water
- 3 limes, chopped
- 50 g (1.75 oz.) chopped mango
- 150 ml (5 oz.) white rum
- 50 g (1.75 oz.) pineapple pieces
- 2 mint sprigs
- Ice cubes

PREPARATION

1. Put the mango, limes and pineapple in a jug with the sugar, and muddle together.
2. Add the mint leaves.
3. Top with ice.
4. Pour the pineapple rum and the white rum, and top up with some sparkling water.

STORMY CAFFEINATED COCKTAIL

Difficulty: Easy ¦ Kcal: 145 ¦ Carbs: 7 g
Sugars: 7 g ¦ Gluten Free

INGREDIENTS

- 25 ml (0.85 oz.) dark rum
- 2 tbsp freshly brewed espresso
- 25 ml (0.85 oz.) tequila
- Ginger beer
- Ice cubes

PREPARATION

1. Fill a glass with ice.
2. Pour the tequila and rum.
3. Top with ginger beer.
4. Pour in the espresso before serving.

RHUBARB GIN

Difficulty: Easy ¦ Kcal: 63 ¦ Carbs: 7 g
Sugars: 7 g ¦ Gluten-Free ¦ Vegan

INGREDIENTS

- 400 g (14 oz.) caster sugar
- 1 kg (35 oz.) pink rhubarb stalks
- 800 ml (27 oz.) gin

PREPARATION

1. Wash the rhubarb, trim the stalks and get rid of the base and all leaves.
2. Cut the rhubarb stalks into pieces and put in a big jar with the sugar.
3. Shake everything and leave to rest overnight.
4. After about 24 hours, you can add the gin and shake the mixture once again.
5. Leave to rest for at least 4 weeks before serving.

PINK NEGRONI

Difficulty: Easy ¦ Kcal: 140 ¦ Carbs: 9 g
Sugars: 8 g ¦ Vegan

INGREDIENTS

- 35 ml (1.2 oz.) pink gin
- 15 ml (0.5 oz.) Aperol
- 25 ml (0.85 oz.) rose vermouth
- Ice cubes
- Some wedges of pink grapefruit, to garnish
- 1 basil leaf, to garnish

PREPARATION

1. Pour the Aperol, pink gin and vermouth in a tumbler along with ice. Stir well.
2. Add some pink grapefruit wedges and a basil leaf to garnish, before serving.

PORNSTAR MARTINI

Difficulty: Easy ¦ Kcal: 224 ¦ Carbs: 16 g
Sugars: 16 g ¦ Gluten-Free ¦ Vegetarian

INGREDIENTS

- 60 ml (2 oz.) vanilla vodka
- the seeds of 1 passion fruit
- 30 ml (1 oz.) passoa
- 1 tbsp sugar syrup
- 1 tbsp lime juice
- 1 ripe passion fruit, to serve
- Prosecco, to serve

PREPARATION

1. Add the passion fruit seeds into a cocktail shaker.
2. Add the passoa, lime juice, vodka, and sugar syrup, along with ice. Shack well.
3. Pour the cocktail into 2 martini glasses.
4. Top up with the prosecco, and add ½ passion fruit to garnish.

FROZEN STRAWBERRY DAIQUIRI

Difficulty: Easy ¦ Kcal: 219 ¦ Carbs: 17 g
Sugars: 17 g ¦ Gluten-free ¦ Vegan

INGREDIENTS

- 100 ml (3.4 oz.) rum
- 200 g (6.8 oz.) ice
- 500 g (17 oz.) strawberries
- The juice of ½ lime
- Lime slices, to garnish
- 1 strawberry, halved, to garnish

PREPARATION

1. Blend the strawberries until you get a creamy texture, and remove all seeds.
2. Put the puree into the blender with rum, lime juice, and ice.
3. Divide the blended mixture between 2 Martini glasses.
4. Garnish with lime slices and strawberry halves.

ELDERFLOWER AND HERBS COOLER

Difficulty: Easy ¦ Kcal: 243 ¦ Carbs: 15 g
Sugars: 15 g ¦ Gluten-free ¦ Vegan

INGREDIENTS

- 150 ml (5 oz.) elderflower liqueur
- 50 ml (1.7 oz.) elderflower cordial
- 150 ml (5 oz.) gin
- 8 edible flowers
- 330 ml (11.1 oz.) sparkling water
- 2 rosemary sprigs, leaves only
- 2 thyme sprigs, leaves only
- Ice cubes

PREPARATION

1. Fill the holes of an ice cubes tray with flowers, water and herbs. Leave in the freezer until frozen.
2. Pour the gin, elderflower liqueur and elderflower cordial into a large jug along with some ice cubes. Stir well.
3. Pour into 4 tall glasses.
4. Top with soda and garnish with some floral ice cubes.

APPLE, ELDERFLOWER AND GIN

Difficulty: Easy ¦ Kcal: 208 ¦ Carbs: 31 g
Sugars: 31 g ¦ Vegetarian

INGREDIENTS

- 250 ml (8.5 oz.) gin
- 1 l (33. 8 oz.) apple juice
- 200 ml (6.7 oz.) elderflower cordial
- Apple slices, to garnish
- Ice cubes, to garnish

PREPARATION

1. Mix the cordial with the gin.
2. Pour the cocktail into 8 glasses.
3. Top up with apple juice.
4. Garnish with apple slices and some ice cubes.

FROZEN MARGARITA

Difficulty: Easy ¦ Kcal: 232 ¦ Carbs: 16 g
Sugars: 16 g ¦ Gluten-Free ¦ Vegan

INGREDIENTS

- 25 ml (0.85 oz.) lime juice
- 50 ml (1.70 oz.) tequila
- 25 ml (0.85 oz.) Cointreau
- 15 ml (0.50 oz.) sugar syrup
- Ice cubes
- A couple of wedges of lime, to garnish

PREPARATION

1. Put all the ingredients in a blender.
2. Shake until smooth.
3. Serve into a margarita glass and garnish with the lime wedges.

PIÑA COLADA

Difficulty: Easy ¦ Kcal: 314 ¦ Carbs: 14.3 g
Sugars: 13.6 g

INGREDIENTS

- 60 ml (2 oz.) white rum
- 120 ml (4 oz.) pineapple juice
- 60 ml (2 oz.) coconut cream
- Pineapple wedges, to garnish

PREPARATION

1. Process all the ingredients along with some ice in a blender, until you get a smooth texture.
2. Pour into a tall glass.
3. Garnish with some pineapple wedges.

WOO WOO

Difficulty: Easy ¦ Kcal: 195 ¦ Carbs: 13 g
Sugars: 13 g ¦ Gluten-Free ¦ Vegan

INGREDIENTS

- 100 ml (3.4 oz.) cranberry juice
- 50 ml (1.7 oz.) vodka
- The juice of ½ lemon
- 24 ml (0.8 oz.) peach schnapps
- Ice cubes
- Lime wedges

PREPARATION

1. Put all the liquid ingredients, the lime juice and some ice into your cocktail shaker, and shake well.
2. Strain the cocktail into a tumbler, and add additional ice.
3. Garnish with lime wedges before serving.

STRAWBERRY MOJITO

Difficulty: Easy ¦ Kcal: 179 ¦ Carbs: 9 g
Sugars: 8 g ¦ Gluten-Free ¦ Vegetarian

INGREDIENTS

- 350 ml (11.8oz.) white rum
- 2 limes, chopped
- 600 ml (20.3 oz.) sparkling water
- Black pepper
- 2 tbsp granulated sugar
- Ice cubes
- 2 mint sprigs, with leaves
- 10 strawberries

PREPARATION

1. In a jug, mix the strawberries, sugar and limes until you get a creamy texture.
2. Bruise some mint leaves and add to the strawberry mixture, along with some black pepper.
3. Stir in the sparkling water and the rum.
4. Serve with ice cubes.

VODKA AND CRANBERRY BLUSH

Difficulty: Easy ¦ Kcal: 0 ¦ Carbs: 0 g
Sugars: 0 g

INGREDIENTS

- 600 ml (20.3 oz.) cranberry juice
- 200 ml (6.8 oz.) vodka
- 200 ml (6.8 oz.) vodka Cointreau
- 400 ml (13.5 oz.) orange juice
- Crushed ice
- Lime peel

PREPARATION

1. Pour both the Cointreau and the vodka into a jug.
2. Add the orange and cranberry juices and stir well.
3. Fill 12 glasses with your cocktails and some crushed ice.
4. Garnish with lime peel.

WATERMELON GIN SPRITZER

Difficulty: Easy ¦ Kcal: 0 ¦ Carbs: 0 g
Sugars: 0 g

INGREDIENTS

- 100 g (3.4 oz.) watermelon, chopped
- 2 limes, cut into pieces
- 2 tbsp gin
- Tonic water

PREPARATION

1. Squeeze a couple of pieces of lime into 8 cocktail glasses, and drop in the flesh.
2. Divide the watermelon pieces among the glasses.
3. Add some ice cubes, along with the gin.
4. Top up with tonic water.

ORANGE AND CARDAMOM MARTINI

Difficulty: Easy ¦ Kcal: 246 ¦ Carbs: 14 g
Sugars: 14 g

INGREDIENTS

- 400 ml (13.5 oz.) vodka
- 12 cardamom pods
- 125 ml (4.2 oz.) Cointreau
- 6 tbsp Seville orange marmalade
- 4 tbsp lemon juice
- Ice cubes

PREPARATION

1. Bash ½ of the cardamom pods with a mortar.
2. In a pan over medium heat, whisk the vodka with the marmalade. Stir in the crushed cardamom pods. Turn the heat off before the mixture starts boiling. Leave to infuse for about ½ hour, then strain.
3. Add the lemon juice and Cointreau, then store into the fridge for a while.
4. Serve with additional marmalade and ice, and extra cardamom pods on top.

DRIVER'S PUNCH

Difficulty: Easy ¦ Kcal: 56 ¦ Carbs: 14 g
Sugars: 1 g

INGREDIENTS

- 600 ml (20.3 oz.) Appletiser (or any other sparkling apple juice)
- 100 ml (3.4 oz.) cranberry juice
- 100 g (3.4 oz) cranberry
- 500 ml (16.9 oz.) blood orange juice
- Lime wedges
- Orange wedges
- Mint sprigs
- The juice of 1 lime

PREPARATION

1. Cover the cranberries with water and freeze until solid.
2. Meanwhile, mix the orange and lime juices with the cranberry juice in a jug.
3. Smash the frozen cranberries and put in the bottom of eight glasses.
4. Add 1 wedge of lime and 1 wedge of orange into each glass, along with some meant leaves.
5. Pour the mixed fruit juices and top up the cocktail with Appletiser.

ROSE AND STRAWBERRY COCKTAIL

Difficulty: Easy ¦ Kcal: 244 ¦ Carbs: 32 g
Sugars: 32 g

INGREDIENTS

- 50 g (1.7 oz.) caster sugar
- 100 g (3.4 oz.) strawberries
- Champagne or prosecco
- 2 tbsp rosewater

PREPARATION

1. Process the sugar, strawberries and rosewater in a blender until you get a puree.
2. Serve into cocktail glasses.
3. Top up with Champagne or Prosecco.

PINK GIN ICED TEA

Difficulty: Easy ¦ Kcal: 136 ¦ Carbs: 13 g
Sugars: 11 g ¦ Gluten-Free ¦ Vegetarian

INGREDIENTS

- 100 ml (3.4 oz.) pink gin
- 100 ml (3.4 oz.) pink grapefruit juice
- 100 ml (3.4 oz.) elderflower cordial
- 1 chamomile tea bag
- 100 ml (3.4 oz.) spiced rum
- Ice cubes
- Thyme sprigs for garnishing

PREPARATION

1. Brew the tea bag in boiling water, and steep following the instructions on the packaging. Once ready, leave to cool.
2. Pour the remaining ingredients into a jug.
3. Add the ice cubes and the chamomile, and stir well. Stir in the tea.
4. Garnish with thyme sprigs.

EASTERN BREEZE

Difficulty: Easy ¦ Kcal: 167 ¦ Carbs: 11 g
Sugars: 11 g ¦ Gluten-Free ¦ Vegan

INGREDIENTS

- 600 ml (20.2 oz.) apple juice
- 300 ml (10.1 oz.) vodka
- Ice cubes
- Mint leaves
- The seeds from 1 pomegranate

PREPARATION

1. Fill six wine glasses with ice.
2. Pour the vodka into each class and fill with the apple juice.
3. Garnish with mint leaves and pomegranate seeds before serving.

BLUEBERRY MOJITO

Difficulty: Easy ¦ Kcal: 173 ¦ Carbs: 8 g
Sugars: 8 g ¦ Gluten-Free ¦ Vegan

INGREDIENTS

- 3 lemons, chopped
- 350 ml (11.8 oz.) white rum
- 100 g (3.4 oz.) blueberries
- 600 ml (20.2 oz.) sparkling water
- 2 bruised mint sprigs, with leaves
- 2 tbsp granulated sugar

PREPARATION

1. In a jar, muddle the lemons, blueberries and sugar together to get a syrup-like mixture.
2. Add the mint leaves and some ice cubes to the jar.
3. Pour the water and the rum, and stir everything together.

ELDERFLOWER AND CUCUMBER GIN TONIC

Difficulty: Easy ¦ Kcal: 199 ¦ Carbs: 33 g
Sugars: 17 g ¦ Gluten Free

INGREDIENTS

- 100 ml (3.4 oz.) elderflower cordial
- 1 cucumber
- 100 ml (3.4 oz.) gin
- Tonic water, to top up

PREPARATION

1. Grate the cucumber into a sieve or piece of kitchen paper over a bowl. Press down with a spoon to extract all the juice.
2. Add the gin and the elderflower cordial to the cucumber juice.
3. Pour everything into your cocktail glasses.
4. Top up with tonic water.
5. Serve with strips of cucumber.

SUMMER PUNCH

Difficulty: Easy ¦ Kcal: 177 ¦ Carbs: 16 g
Sugars: 16 g ¦ Gluten-Free ¦ Vegan

INGREDIENTS

- 250 ml (8.5 oz.) vodka
- 250 ml (8.5 oz.) elderflower liqueur
- 500 ml (17 oz.) apple juice
- 125 ml (4.2 oz.) sparkling water
- 125 ml (4.2 oz.) lemon juice
- 50 g (1.7 oz.) caster sugar
- Ice Cubes
- Lemon, to serve
- Fresh herbs, like mint and basil, to serve

PREPARATION

1. Mix the sugar and lemon juice in a bowl. Stir well until the sugar is dissolved.
2. Transfer to a serving bowl along with all the other liquid ingredients.
3. Fill with ice cubes and stir once again.
4. Serve with lemon slices and herbs.

MAI TAI

Difficulty: Easy ¦ Kcal: 284 ¦ Carbs: 19.6 g
Sugars: 16.6 g

INGREDIENTS

- 1 tbsp grenadine
- 2 tbsp white rum
- 2 tbsp triple sec
- 2 tbsp dark rum
- 1 tbsp almond syrup
- The juice of ½ lime
- 1 maraschino cherry

PREPARATION

1. Mix all the ingredients in a cocktail shaker.
2. Serve in a tumbler with ice cubes.
3. Garnish with a cherry before serving.

SIDECAR

Difficulty: Easy ¦ Kcal: 239 ¦ Carbs: 18 g
Sugars: 18 g ¦ Gluten-free ¦ Egg-free ¦ Vegan

INGREDIENTS

- 50 ml (1.7 oz.) cognac
- 25 ml (0.85 oz.) lemon juice
- 25 ml (0.85) triple sec
- Ice cubes
- Angostura bitters, to garnish

PREPARATION

1. Put all the ingredients into a cocktail shaker.
2. Leave a couple of glasses in the refrigerator to chill for a few hours.
3. Shake the cocktail well, then pour it into the chilled coupe glass.
4. Serve with a dash of Angostura bitters.

SLOE GIN

Difficulty: Medium ¦ Kcal: 198 ¦ Carbs: 13 g
Sugars: 13 g ¦ Gluten-Free ¦ Vegan

INGREDIENTS

- 50 ml (1.7 oz.) sloe gin
- 25 ml (0.8 oz.) gin
- 25 ml (0.8 oz.) lemon juice
- Ice cubes
- Crushed ice

Juniper Syrup

- 1 tbsp juniper berries
- 100 g (3.4 oz.) white caster sugar

PREPARATION

1. You can start by making the syrup. Bring to the boil the sugar with 100 ml (3.4 oz.) of water, then add the juniper berries. Once ready, muddle with a spoon or a potato masher.
2. Add all the ingredients (without the crushed ice) into your cocktail shaker and shake well.
3. Serve the cocktail into a tumbler or a glass filled with crushed ice.

NEW YORK SOUR

Difficulty: Medium ¦ Kcal: 191 ¦ Carbs: 11 g
Sugars: 10 g ¦ Gluten-Free ¦ Vegetarian

INGREDIENTS

- 25 ml (8.5 oz.) lemon juice
- 20 ml (0.7 oz.) red wine
- 2 tsp maple syrup
- 50 ml (1.7 oz.) rye whiskey
- 1 tbsp egg white
- Dash orange bitters
- Ice cubes

PREPARATION

1. Pour the maple syrup, lemon juice, bitters, and whisky into a cocktail shaker.
2. Whisk the egg and add it to the shaker.
3. Shake well until everything is well combined.
4. Add some ice and shake again.
5. Pour the cocktail into a tall glass filled with additional ice.
6. Add the red wine slowly and serve the cocktail.

BERGAMOT MOJITO

Difficulty: Medium ¦ Kcal: 264 ¦ Carbs: 51 g
Sugars: 51 g ¦ Gluten-Free ¦ Vegan

INGREDIENTS

- 150 ml (5 oz.) golden rum
- 300 g (10 oz.) golden caster sugar
- The juice of 6 limes
- 12 mint leaves
- The juice of 1 bergamot
- The zest of 1 bergamot

PREPARATION

1. Bring 1 ltr (33 oz.) water to the boil. Stir in the sugar, then leave to cool.
2. Blend the lime juice, mint, and bergamot juice and zest in a food processor.
3. Mix the bergamot mixture with the cooled sugar syrup. Freeze into a plastic container.
4. Scoop the bergamot granita and serve it into chilled cocktail glasses filled with rum.

HURRICANE COCKTAIL

Difficulty: Medium ¦ Kcal: 215 ¦ Carbs: 24 g
Sugars: 22 g ¦ Gluten-Free ¦ Vegan

INGREDIENTS

- 1 passion fruit
- 50 ml (1.7 oz.) dark rum
- 50 ml (1.7 oz.) sugar syrup
- 50 ml (1.7 oz.) white rum
- 2 tsp grenadine
- The juice of 1 orange
- The juice of 1 lemon
- 2 orange slices, to garnish
- 4 cocktail cherries, to garnish

PREPARATION

1. Put the ice and the rums into a cocktail shaker. Add the passion fruit, with the juice of one orange and one lemon.
2. Add the grenadine and sugar syrup, then shake well.
3. Pour the cocktail into two glasses filled with wine.
4. Serve with additional ice, orange slices and some cocktail cherries.

CUCUMBER, MINT AND MELON PUNCH

Difficulty: Medium ¦ Kcal: 251 ¦ Carbs: 34 g
Sugars: 34 g

INGREDIENTS

- 1 l (33.8 oz.) sparkling water
- 500 ml (16.9 oz.) vodka
- 200 g (6.8 oz.) white caster sugar
- 1 large cucumber, chopped
- 1 small bunch mint, without leaves
- 1 small melon
- The juice of 6 limes
- Lime wedges

PREPARATION

1. Put half the mint and the cucumber in a jug. Pour over your vodka. Cover and refrigerate for at least 24 hours. Once ready to use, strain the mixture through a fine sieve.
2. Pour the prepared cucumber and mint-infused vodka and the sugar into a jug and stir well.
3. With a melon baller, scoop some melon balls and drop them into the jug. Leave to steep for ½ hour in the refrigerator.
4. Top up with the sparkling water.
5. Garnish with lime wedges and mint leaves.

CAIPIRINHAS PINEAPPLE

Difficulty: Medium ¦ Kcal: 433 ¦ Carbs: 80 g
Sugars: 77 g

INGREDIENTS

- 400 ml (13 oz.) cachaça liqueur, or light rum
- 1 pineapple
- 800 ml (27 oz.) pineapple juice
- The juice 4 limes
- 8 tbsp golden caster sugar
- Fresh mint
- Crushed ice

PREPARATION

1. Cut the pineapple into chunks.
2. Put part of the pineapple chunks, half the mint, sugar and the lime juice into a pitcher. Smash the ingredients with a wooden spoon.
3. Add the cachaça and some crushed ice.
4. Pour the drink into 8 glasses with more crushed ice.
5. Top up with the pineapple juice.
6. Garnish with mint sprigs and additional pieces of pineapple.

CLARIDGE'S SAZERAC

Difficulty: Medium ¦ Kcal: 119 ¦ Carbs: 7 g
Sugars: 3 g ¦ Gluten-Free ¦ Dairy-free ¦ Vegan

INGREDIENTS

- 30 ml (1 oz.) cognac
- 30 ml (1 oz.) rye whiskey
- 2 drops of absinthe
- 5 ml (0.17 oz.) sugar syrup
- 2 drops of Peychaud's bitters
- Lemon peel, to garnish

PREPARATION

1. Refrigerate a tumbler. Once it is freezing cold, pour the absinthe into it. You need to swirl the tumbler so that the absinthe can cover all its sides.
2. Pour all the remaining ingredients, except for the lemon peel, into a mixing glass. Stir well and pour into the tumbler.
3. Garnish with lemon peel

EARL GREY MARTINI

Difficulty: Medium ┆ Kcal: 5 ┆ Carbs: 0 g
Sugars: 0 g ┆ Gluten-Free ┆ Vegan

INGREDIENTS

- 700 ml (23.7 oz.) bottle of decent gin
- 1 tbsp loose-leaf Earl Grey tea (or 1 teabag)
- Ice cubes

PREPARATION

1. Prepare your tea as usual, and allow it to chill.
2. Pour it in a large jug and stir in the gin. Mix well.
3. Using a coffee filter or a tea strainer, filter all the tea leaves and particles from the drink.
4. Serve over ice.

BLOOD ORANGE STAR ANISE FIZZ

Difficulty: Challenging ¦ Kcal: 170 ¦ Carbs: 12 g
Sugars: 12 g ¦ Gluten Free

INGREDIENTS

- 120 ml (4 oz.) Grand Marnier
- 4 blood oranges, quartered
- 4 tsp tequila
- 1 star anise
- Prosecco, to top up

PREPARATION

1. Soak the blood orange in Grand Marnier for 3 hours. Save about 20 ml (0.7 oz.) of Grand Mardier for later.
2. Place the oranges and their soaking liquid into the oven at 200 C (400 F) and roast with the star anise for 30 minutes, or until caramelised.
3. Once ready, remove the star anise and the skin of the orange, and puree the fruit into a food processor.
4. Mix part of this puree with tequila and Grand Marnier, top with prosecco and serve into cocktail classes.

RHUBARB CUSTARD COCKTAIL

Difficulty: Challenging ¦ Kcal: 126 ¦ Carbs: 10 g
Sugars: 10 g

INGREDIENTS

- 100 ml (3.4 oz.) vodka
- 30 ml (1 oz.) advocaat
- 75 ml (2.5 oz.) lemonade
- 1 rhubarb

Rhubarb Syrup

- 85 g (2.9 oz.) caster sugar
- 300 g (10.1 oz.) chopped rhubarb

PREPARATION

1. First, you need to make the rhubarb syrup. Heat the sugar with 75 ml (2.5 oz.) water and stir until it dissolves. Stir in the chopped rhubarb and bring to a boil. Cook until the rhubarb is very tender.
2. Once ready, transfer the rhubarb mixture into a bowl. Use a wooden spoon to squeeze all the juices out the rhubarb. Bring back the mixture into a saucepan over low heat and stir until you get a syrupy mixture.
3. Pour into a medium jug and wait until it cools completely. Meanwhile, chill 4 cocktail glasses in the freezer.
4. Shake 2/3 of the rhubarb syrup with the vodka and some ice cubes.
5. In another jug, whisk the lemonade, advocaat and ice.
6. Divide the rhubarb mixture between the 4 chilled glasses. Top with the advocaat mixture.
7. Garnish with additional rhubarb shreds.

WINE COCKTAILS

BELLINI

Difficulty: Easy ¦ Kcal: 143 ¦ Carbs: 18 g
Sugars: 18 g

INGREDIENTS

- 1 bottle Prosecco
- 500 ml (16.9 oz.) peach puree

PREPARATION

1. Fill 1/3 of a Champagne flute with the peach puree.
2. Top up with Prosecco.

ORANGE BLOSSOM BELLINI

Difficulty: Easy ¦ Kcal: 106 ¦ Carbs: 4 g
Sugars: 4 g

INGREDIENTS

- 175 ml (5.9 oz.) blood orange juice
- Prosecco
- 1 tbsp orange blossom water

PREPARATION

1. Mix the orange blossom water with the orange juice.
2. Pour into 6 cocktail glasses.
3. Top up with Prosecco.

SPARKLING MINT AND LEMON JULEPS

Difficulty: Easy ¦ Kcal: 0 ¦ Carbs: 0 g
Sugars: 0 g

INGREDIENTS

- 1 bottle of Cava (or any other sparkling wine)
- 4 tbsp fresh lemon juice
- 85 g (2.9 oz.) golden caster sugar
- Fresh mint

PREPARATION

1. Heat the sugar and lemon juice in a saucepan. Let simmer for a couple of minutes, or until you get a syrupy texture. Once ready, leave to cool.
2. Pour the lemon syrup into six Champagne flutes when you are ready to serve your cocktail.
3. Top up with sparkling wine.
4. Garnish with mint leaves.

GOOSEBERRY AND ELDERFLOWER FIZZ

Difficulty: Easy ¦ Kcal: 256 ¦ Carbs: 38 g
Sugars: 38 g

INGREDIENTS

- 3 tbsp elderflower cordial
- 12 gooseberries
- The juice ½ lemon
- 1 tbsp caster sugar
- Prosecco (or any other sparkling wine), to top up

PREPARATION

1. Mush the sugar and the gooseberries into a large jar.
2. Add cordial, lemon juice, and ice cubes. Close the jar lid and shake well.
3. Pour into glasses.
4. Top up with the Prosecco before serving.

PINK GRAPEFRUIT PUNCH

Difficulty: Easy ¦ Kcal: 57 ¦ Carbs: 3 g
Sugars: 2 g ¦ Gluten Free

INGREDIENTS

- 100 ml (3.4 oz.) gin
- 200 ml (6.8 oz.) pink grapefruit juice
- 50 ml (1.7 oz.) Campari
- 750 ml (25.4 oz.) rose wine
- 25 ml (0.85 oz.) red vermouth
- ½ bunch of thyme
- 1 tbsp honey
- Ice cubes

PREPARATION

1. Pour all the ingredients in a punch bowl.
2. Add ice and stir gently.
3. Garnish with thyme.

APPLE PROSECCO PUNCH

Difficulty: Easy ¦ Kcal: 88 ¦ Carbs: 6 g
Sugars: 5 g ¦ Gluten Free

INGREDIENTS

- 400 ml (13.5 oz.) apple juice
- 200 ml (6.8 oz.) vodka
- The juice of 2 lemons
- 750 ml (25.3 oz.) prosecco
- 1 lemon, sliced
- 1 apple, cored and finely sliced
- Ice cubes

PREPARATION

1. Pour the vodka, lemon and apple juice into a punch bowl. Store in the fridge for 2 hours.
2. Top with the Prosecco before serving.
3. Garnish with ice, lemon and apple slices.

ST. NICKS FLIP

Difficulty: Easy ¦ Kcal: 236 ¦ Carbs: 8 g
Sugars: 4 g ¦ Gluten-Free ¦

INGREDIENTS

- 150 ml (5 oz.) muscat wine
- 120 ml (4 oz.) double cream
- 200 ml (6.8 oz.) cognac
- 6 egg whites
- 60 ml (2 oz.) simple syrup
- Ice cubes
- 6 cloves, to garnish
- 6 strips of orange peel, to garnish
- Ground cinnamon, to garnish

PREPARATION

1. Save the cloves, orange peel and cinnamon for later.
2. Mix 1/3 of the remaining ingredients with some ice into a cocktail shaker.
3. Pour into two wine glasses.
4. Repeat with the remaining 2/3 of your ingredients, adding fresh ice each time.
5. Garnish each glass with clove, pared orange and a pinch of cinnamon.

PEACH PUNCH

Difficulty: Easy ¦ Kcal: 161 ¦ Carbs: 16 g
Sugars: 16 g ¦ Dairy-free ¦ Vegetarian

INGREDIENTS

- 1 l (33.4 oz.) soda water
- 150 ml (5 oz.) peach schnapps
- 750 ml (25.4 oz.) rosé wine
- ½ lemon, sliced
- 1 peach, sliced
- 4 tbsp caster sugar
- The zest and juice 1½ lemon
- Ice cubes

PREPARATION

1. Heat the lemon zest and sugar with 100 ml (3.4 oz.) water in a saucepan. Leave to cool, then pour into a jug.
2. Stir in the wine, schnapps, and lemon juice.
3. Top with the soda and serve with ice and fruits.

MELON CUCUMBER PUNCH

Difficulty: Easy ¦ Kcal: 58 ¦ Carbs: 3 g
Sugars: 3 g ¦ Gluten Free

INGREDIENTS

- 1 melon, cut in half
- The juice of 1 lemon
- 100 ml (3.4 oz.) Pimm's
- 50 ml (1.7 oz.) orange liqueur
- 750 ml (23.4 oz.) white wine
- ½ cucumber, sliced
- 1 mint sprig
- 300 ml (10.1 oz.) sparkling water
- Ice cubes

PREPARATION

1. Cut the melon into spheres with a melon baller and fill a large punch bowl.
2. Add the white wine, orange liqueur, lemon juice and Pimm's. Leave to chill in the refrigerator for 2 hours.
3. Top with sparkling water and ice cubes.
4. Serve with mint sprigs and cucumber pieces.

BICYCLETTE

Difficulty: Easy ¦ Kcal: 184 ¦ Carbs: 2 g
Sugars: 1 g ¦ Gluten Free

INGREDIENTS

- 200 ml (6.8 oz.) dry white wine
- 100 ml (3.4 oz.) Campari
- 4-5 Ice cubes
- ½ lemon (sliced)

PREPARATION

1. Pour the Campari into 2 glasses wine.
2. Add a couple of ice cubes.
3. Top with white wine.
4. Garnish with lemon wedges and stir before serving.

CASSIS SPRITZ

Difficulty: Easy ¦ Kcal: 165 ¦ Carbs: 11 g
Sugars: 11 g ¦ Vegetarian

INGREDIENTS

- 30 ml (1 oz.) white wine
- 15 ml (0.5 oz.) crème de cassis
- 30 ml (1 oz.) Cynar
- Ice cubes
- Soda water, to taste
- 1 sprig of thyme, to garnish

PREPARATION

1. Put the ice cubes into a wine glass.
2. Pour in all your liquid ingredients and stir gently.
3. Add the soda water.
4. Garnish with the thyme before serving.

SPICED APPLE SNAPS FIZZ

Difficulty: Easy ¦ Kcal: 169 ¦ Carbs: 11 g
Sugars: 11 g ¦ Gluten Free

INGREDIENTS

- 200 ml (6.8 oz.) bottle sparkling wine
- 50 ml (1.7 oz.) gin
- 4 tbsp apple juice
- The juice of 1 lemon
- Ice cubes
- Ground cinnamon
- ½ small apple, thinly sliced

PREPARATION

1. Pour the gin into a cocktail shaker.
2. Add the apple and lemon juices, some cinnamon and ice. Shake well.
3. Pour into 2 fluted glasses.
4. Add the sparkling wine.
5. Top up with additional cinnamon and garnish with the apple slices.

COCO VIZ

Difficulty: Easy ¦ Kcal: 110 ¦ Carbs: 4 g
Sugars: 4 g ¦ Gluten Free

INGREDIENTS

- 25 ml (0.8 oz.) coconut rum
- 50 ml (1.7 oz.) coconut water
- The juice of ½ lime
- Ice cubes
- 50 ml (1.7 oz.) prosecco

PREPARATION

1. Add all the ingredients (without the Prosecco) into a cocktail shaker and shake well.
2. Pour the cocktail into a chilled couple of glasses.
3. Top with Prosecco and serve immediately.

EL VERMOUTH SANGRIA

Difficulty: Easy ¦ Kcal: 172 ¦ Carbs: 18 g
Sugars: 17 g ¦ Gluten-Free ¦ Dairy-free ¦ Egg-free ¦ Vegan

INGREDIENTS

- 1 bottle red wine
- 1 banana, sliced
- 1 orange, sliced
- 1 pear, sliced
- 1 lemon, sliced
- 200 ml (6.8 oz.) sweet red vermouth
- 200 ml (6.8 oz.) lemonade
- 420 g (14.2 oz.) canned peaches with syrup, cut into thin slices
- Ice cubes
- Lemon and orange slices, to garnish

PREPARATION

1. Pour all the fruits in a pitcher with the syrup from the peaches' can. Mix well with a wooden spoon.
2. Add the vermouth, mix again, then add the red wine.
3. Fill in with ice cubes. Pour in the lemonade and stir well.
4. Garnish with lemon and orange slices.

TRADITIONAL MULLED WINE

Difficulty: Medium ¦ Kcal: 182 ¦ Carbs: 23 g
Sugars: 11 g

INGREDIENTS

- 1 l (33.8 oz.) apple juice
- 125 ml (4.2 oz.) red wine
- 3 tbsp Cointreau
- 115 g (3.8 oz.) caster sugar
- 2 stars anise
- 1 cinnamon stick, halved
- 3 small apples, thinly sliced
- 100 g (3.4) frozen fruits

PREPARATION

1. Pour the apple juice and wine into a saucepan. Stir in the cinnamon stick, sugar, and star anise. Keep stirring until the sugar dissolves, then cook for another 15 minutes.
2. Once ready, you can serve it in a mug. Stir in the Cointreau, some apple slices and the frozen fruits.

COINTREAU MULLED WINE

Difficulty: Medium ¦ Kcal: 236 ¦ Carbs: 25 g
Sugars: 25 g

INGREDIENTS

- 150 ml (5 oz.) water
- 750 ml (25.4 oz.) light red wine
- 100 g (3.4 oz.) muscovado sugar
- 4 cloves
- 1 lemon
- 1 cinnamon stick
- 2 clementine
- Orange zest, to garnish
- Additional star anise, to garnish

PREPARATION

1. Heat 100 g (3.4 oz.) of sugar in a saucepan along with the cinnamon stick, 1 star anise, the cloves, and the water. Bring to the boil, and stir until the sugar has dissolved.
2. Leave the syrup to simmer, then transfer to a larger jug and leave to cool.
3. Slice 1 lemon and 2 clementines and add to the syrup, along with the wine and Cointreau. Stir well and leave to chill for at least 2 hours.
4. Once ready to be served, garnish the cocktail with ice, a twist of orange zest and additional star anise. if you want, you can warm the drink once again to serve it hot, without the ice.

CHOCOLATE COCKTAIL RECIPES

CHOCOLATE MARTINI

Difficulty: Easy ¦ Kcal: 327 ¦ Carbs: 25 g
Sugars: 24 g ¦ Vegetarian

INGREDIENTS

- 1 tsp chocolate powder
- 100 (3.4 oz.) ml vodka
- 50 ml (1.7 oz.) coffee liqueur
- 50 ml (1.7 oz.) Irish cream liqueur
- 1 tbsp chocolate syrup
- Ice cubes

PREPARATION

1. Melt the chocolate and brush it on the side of two glasses. Store into the refrigerator for a few hours.
2. Pour the coffee and Irish liqueurs, vodka, and chocolate syrup into a cocktail shaker with some ice. Shake well.
3. Serve the drink into the chilled glasses.

JACKSON CHOCOLATE ORANGE

Difficulty: Easy ¦ Kcal: 232 ¦ Carbs: 19 g
Sugars: 18 g

INGREDIENTS

- 100 ml (3.4 oz.) vodka
- 100 ml (3.4 oz.) crème de cacao
- 60 ml (2 oz.) orange syrup
- 100 g (3.4 oz.) golden caster sugar
- 40 ml (1.35 oz.) orange juice
- The zest of 1 orange
- Ice cubes
- Grated dark chocolate, to garnish

PREPARATION

1. The first step is to prepare the orange syrup. Combine the golden caster sugar and the orange zest with 100 ml (3.4 oz.) of water, and bring to the boil. Stir well until you obtain a smooth texture.
2. Meanwhile, put four glasses to chill in the fridge. Once ready, dip the rims into the grated dark chocolate.
3. Shake all the remaining liquid ingredients with the orange syrup and some ice, and then pour the cocktail into your glasses.

CHOCOLATE VODKA SHOTS

Difficulty: Easy ¦ Kcal: 219 ¦ Carbs: 13 g
Sugars: 12 g

INGREDIENTS

- 150 ml (5 oz.) vodka
- 75 ml (2.5 oz.) chocolate cream liqueur
- 1 tsp chocolate spread
- 75 ml (2.5 oz.) hazelnut liqueur
- Ice cubes
- 2 packs of Kinder Bueno, to garnish

PREPARATION

1. Heat the chocolate spread in the microwave, then brush a line of chocolate inside six shot glasses.
2. Pour all the liquid ingredients in a cocktail shaker with ice. Shake well.
3. Strain the cocktail into the shot glasses and decorate the drink with Kinder Bueno chunks before serving.

SALTED CARAMEL RUM HOT CHOCOLATE

Difficulty: Easy ¦ Kcal: 457 ¦ Carbs: 40 g
Sugars: 39 g

INGREDIENTS

- 25 ml (0.85 oz.) dark rum
- 150 ml (5 oz.) whole milk
- 50 g (1.7 oz.) milk chocolate
- 2 tbsp dulce de leche or thick caramel

PREPARATION

1. Mix the dulce de leche and the rum until you get a smooth cream.
2. Warm the milk in a saucepan and stir in the chocolate. Stir well until the chocolate has melted.
3. Turn the heat on once again, and stir in the rum mixture.
4. Season with a bit of salt and serve into a mug.

COCONUT HOT CHOCOLATE

Difficulty: Easy ¦ Kcal: 318 ¦ Carbs: 22 g
Sugars: 21 g

INGREDIENTS

- 25 ml (0.85 oz.) coconut-flavoured rum
- 150 ml (5 oz.) whole milk
- 1 tsp finely grated dark chocolate
- 25 g (0.85 oz.) white chocolate, chopped
- 1 tsp coconut flakes, to garnish

PREPARATION

1. Warm the milk into a saucepan, and stir in the white chocolate. Stir well until the chocolate has melted.
2. Add the rum and then pour everything into your favourite mug.
3. Serve with coconut flakes.

SALTED CARAMEL PECAN SOUR

Difficulty: Medium ¦ Kcal: 358 ¦ Carbs: 12 g
Sugars: 12 g ¦ Gluten Free

INGREDIENTS

- Vodka
- 100 g (3.4 oz.) toasted pecans, chopped
- 120 ml (4 oz.) clementine juice
- 160 g (5.4 oz.) golden caster sugar
- ½ tsp sea salt flakes
- 18 drops chocolate bitters
- Ice cubes
- 3 egg whites
- 6 dehydrated orange slices, to garnish
- Nutmeg powder, to garnish

PREPARATION

1. Heat the pecans, the salt and the sugar with 80 ml (2.7 oz.) water. Leave to cool, then pour through a sieve to separate the pecans.
2. Mix the clementine juice, egg whites, vodka, and the pecan salted caramel syrup with the cocktail shaker until the egg white gains volume.
3. Add ice and shake for further 15 seconds.
4. Strain the drink into coupe glasses.
5. Garnish with dehydrated orange slices and fresh nutmeg.

MUDSLIDE

Difficulty: Medium ¦ Kcal: 656 ¦ Carbs: 26 g
Sugars: 22 g ¦ Gluten-Free ¦ Vegetarian

INGREDIENTS

- 60 ml (2 oz.) Irish cream liqueur
- 60 ml (2 oz.) coffee-flavoured liqueur
- 50 g (1.7 oz.) dark chocolate
- 60 ml (2 oz.) vodka
- 100 ml (3.4 oz.) double cream
- Ice cubes

PREPARATION

1. Melt half of the dark chocolate in the microwave.
2. Refrigerate two small tumblers and, once chilled, dip their rim in the melted chocolate. Leave them to stand upright so that the chocolate melt can drip down the sides, then return to the fridge.
3. Pour the vodka, liqueurs and double cream in a cocktail shaker along with ice. Shake well.
4. Fill the chilled glasses with additional ice, and pour the cocktail.
5. Serve with extra chocolate grated on top.

MINI EGG MARTINI

Difficulty: Medium ¦ Kcal: 425 ¦ Carbs: 32 g
Sugars: 32 g ¦ Gluten Free

INGREDIENTS

- 25 g (0.8 oz.) mini chocolate eggs
- 25 ml (0.8 oz.) Baileys
- 25 ml (0.8 oz.) crème de cacao
- 1 tsp honey
- 50ml vodka
- Ice cubes

PREPARATION

1. Crush the chocolate eggs and place into a plate.
2. Brush the rim of your glass with some honey, then dip it into the crushed chocolate.
3. Store the glass in the refrigerator.
4. Pour the Baileys, crème de cacao and vodka into your cocktail shaker along with ice cubes. Shake well.
5. Serve the cocktail into your chilled glass.

MIDNIGHT HOT CHOCOLATE WITH MINT

Difficulty: Challenging ¦ Kcal: 764 ¦ Carbs: 39 g
Sugars: 34 g

INGREDIENTS

- 50 ml (1.7 oz.) double cream
- 25 ml (0.8 oz.) crème de menthe
- 150 ml (5 oz.) whole milk
- Peppermint extract
- 1 tsp icing sugar
- 50 g (1.7 oz.) dark chocolate, chopped
- Dark chocolate sprinkles, to garnish

PREPARATION

1. Whip the cream. Stir in the peppermint extract and the icing sugar. Store in the fridge.
2. Heat the milk until simmering. Remember to stir frequently!
3. Turn the heat off and add the chocolate. Keep stirring until the chocolate is completely melted, and you obtain a creamy mixture.
4. Rewarm on medium heat and stir in the crème the menthe.
5. Pour into your favourite mug.
6. Top with the whipped mint cream and garnish with dark chocolate sprinkles.
7. Serve while hot.

Printed in Great Britain
by Amazon

75914163R00066